D1458375

VAHAZAR

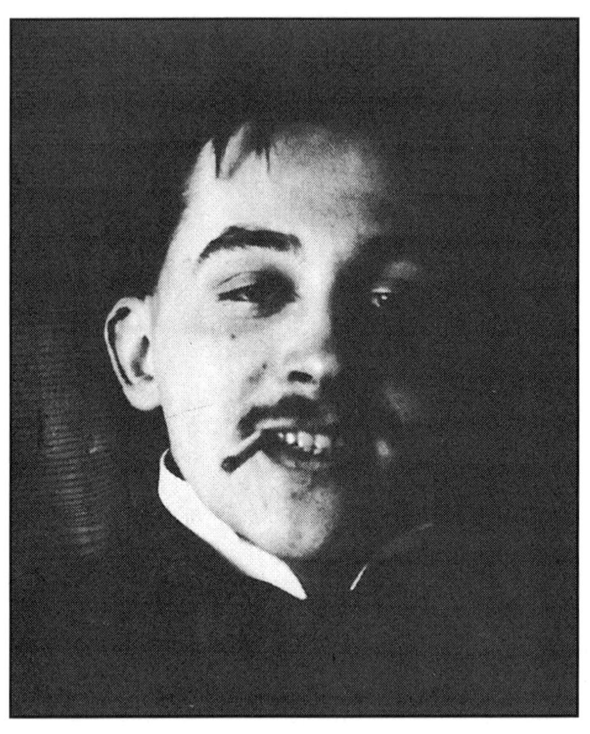

Polish avant-garde playwright Witkacy (1903)

VAHAZAR
OR
ON THE UPLANDS OF ABSURDITY

(Non-Euclidean Drama in Four Acts)

by
Stanisław Ignacy Witkiewicz

Translated from the Polish by
Celina Wieniewska

Adapted by
Patrick Fetherston

With an introduction by
Paul Rosheim

Black Scat Books
2015

First Edition

ISBN-13 978-0-692-51955-4

Cover art & book design: Norman Conquest

BLACK SCAT BOOKS
Sublime Art & Literature
BlackScatBooks.com

Motto:
Es ist doch teuer zu Macht zu kommen – die Macht verdummt.
—Friedrich Nietzche

Dedicated to:
Tadeusz Langier

CONTENTS

WITKACY AND GABERBOCCHUS PRESS

Stanisław Ignacy Witkiewicz (1885-1939) — also known by his pen name "Witkacy," which combined parts of two of his names — was a Polish playwright, novelist, painter, photographer, and philosopher. Between 1918 and 1924, Witkacy wrote more than twenty plays that bridge August Strindberg's plays with those by Samuel Beckett and Eugène Ionesco. His writings often depicted the collapse of an established, decadent order of individuals, only to be replaced by an "anthill of automatons."

A handful of his plays written in 1921, including *Vahazar, or On the Uplands of Absurdity,* exemplified what he called "Pure Form." A personal, metaphysical rebellion against realism and naturalism, Pure Form pursued instead a subjective approach. This style postulated that colors, sounds, and movements were as important as the spoken words of a performance, with the goal of eliminating the constraints of nature and external reality. Ideally, an audience would perceive a Pure Form theatrical performance like a collective dream.

Witkacy apparently was inspired to write *Vahazar* after reading Georges Ribemont-Dessaignes's *The Emperor of China*, a Dada-ist play in free verse about a violent political regime based on mathematics. Alfred Jarry's Ubu, the King of Poland, was another likely model for the Witkacian absolute ruler.

In comparison with his ten previous plays, *Vahazar* exhibits Witkakcy's growing confidence in his dramaturgy. This is his first play where the subject is the daily life in an anthill society, and the stage is filled with swirling, howling mobs. Paranoid and crazed, Vahazar, at the vortex of total power, is trapped in nothingness. Alternating spells of frenzy and lethargy, Vahazar turns to religious cults and pseudo-scientific theories for answers to ontological questions, before finally becoming a martyr. Interested in the dynamic relationship between the oppressor and the oppressed, Witkacy recycled the ancient practice of societal renewal through the ritual killing of the sacred leader by his or her successor, as described in Sir James G. Frazer's *The Golden Bough*. But *Vahazar*, on the verge of nonsense, offers no metaphysical solutions to the enigma of existence.

Witkacy grew up in the shadow of his dominating father, also named Stanisław Witkiewicz. The elder Stanisław was an architect, painter, and art critic, who helped establish Zakopane, where the family lived near the Tatra Mountains, as an artists' colony for many of the leading painters, poets, writers, and composers in Poland. The father believed in home-schooling his precocious only child in accordance with his educational principles. Young Staś began painting, playing the piano, and writing plays at a very early age. Later, against his father's wishes, Witkacy attended the Cracow Academy of Fine Arts for three years before leaving without a degree.

Suffering from a sense of nihilism and heightened emotional states, the multitalented Witkacy felt he was nearing a breakdown in his mid-twenties. Some of this he recorded in *The 622 Downfalls of Bungo; or, The Demonic Woman* (1910-11), an unpublished, autobiographical *roman à clef* about his affair with an older actress, and a homoerotic fantasy involving his best friend, Bronisław Malinowski. Undoubtedly, Witkacy's condition became worse as his fiancée shot herself when he was twenty-eight.

Meanwhile, Malinowski had become an anthropologist and university lecturer in London. In the hope of lessening his friend's despair, he invited Witkacy to accompany him, as a photographer, to a scientific conference in Australia. The expedition, which included a two-week stopover in Ceylon, was fraught with constant bickering and tensions between them. Two weeks after arriving in Australia, any possible recuperation by Witkacy was cut short by the beginning of World War I. Nevertheless this trip allowed Witkacy to contemplate European civilization and customs from an outside perspective, and perhaps to see authoritarian colonial systems as analogous to the oppressive paternal control he had experienced within his family.

Seeking a dramatic change in his life, Witkacy next travelled to Saint Petersburg, where he was accepted into an accelerated army officer training program. In 1916, after five months of training, he was sent to the front where he was promptly wounded. He was either in the hospital or on convalescent leave for the rest of the war. During this period of extended sick leave, he painted portraits and other pictures at a rate in excess of one per day. He spent his commissions on cocaine and peyote. And, surprisingly, following the February Revolution of 1917 and the abolition of officer ranks, his regiment elected him to be its political commissar.

At this point, Witkacy definitely wanted to get out of revolutionary Russia. Most of the social privileges that he had enjoyed were gone after the October Revolution brought the Bolsheviks to power. Being a former Czarist army officer, he was always afraid of being arrested by the Red Guards. This fear remained with him for the rest of his life. After his discharge from the army, he kept a low profile for eight months until 1918, when he was finally able to return to a soon-to-be reconstituted Poland.

Back in Zakopane, and living in his mother's boarding house (his parents had separated, and the father died in 1915), Witkacy now entered into his most productive period of play-writing. The experience of witnessing the fall of a decadent old order, the ensuing chaos, and the radical changes that brought forth a threatening new order became a central theme in Witkacy's writing. Amongst his plays and two later novels, *Vahazar* is the archetype of this theme. Nonetheless, it remained unpublished until 1962, and unperformed until 1965. Only seven of his plays were published in his lifetime. Except for a 1925 touring theater production of one of his more conventional works, his plays were scarcely performed prior to his death (many productions had only one or two performances). Witkacy occasionally tried to stage his own productions at a local hotel, using amateur actors and minimal sets, but these were not taken seriously by critics or audiences, who dismissed him as a sort of prankster.

While hoping to earn money by writing plays, Witkacy actually supported himself by making portraits. He also believed that he could resolve his emotional and financial difficulties with an advantageous marriage. So in 1923 he married Jadwiga Unrug, but only after they had agreed to maintain an "open" arrangement. She lived in her apartment in Warsaw; and he continued to reside at his mother's boarding house, at the same time crisscrossing the country to further his portraiture business.

About this time, having lost his faith in painting as an art, Witkacy resorted to his portrait-painting business as a scheme for money-making. His printed prospectus, "Rules of the S.I. Witkiewicz Portrait-Painting Firm," described the different types of portraits that could be obtained, and their prices, based on the desired degree of alterations of appearance, colors, and other psychedelic effects. Mostly for his friends, Witkacy made portraits of pure, metaphysical sensations while under the influence of drugs. Next to his signature, he encoded the dosage of each drug he had consumed for the sitting.

By the mid-1920s, Witkacy largely had given up writing plays. Instead, he switched genres and published a variety of prose books: two large dystopian novels: *Farewell to Autumn* (1927), and *Insatiability* (1930), both replete with semi-autobiographical digressions; a book about his experiences with certain drugs, *Narcotics: Nicotine, Alcohol, Cocaine, Peyote, Morphine, and Ether* (1932); and his philosophical opus, *The Concepts and Principles Implied by the Idea of Existence* (1935), which sold only twelve copies. Despite his own difficulties, he championed emerging Polish writers Bruno Schulz (doomed author of *The Street of Crocodiles*) and Witold Gombrowicz (who wrote *Ferdydurke* before escaping to Argentina).

Witkacy suffered from suicidal tendencies throughout his life. Creativity, especially employing his Pure Form in plays and portraits, seemed a defense against the ever-present feelings of absurdity and depression. Sadly, his end seemed like something from his novels. After his mother died in 1931, he rented a room in a nearby house owned by his two aunts. With the economic collapse of the 1930s, fewer portraits were commissioned, and money became scarcer. Ultimately, he fled eastward, trapped between the invading totalitarian armies of Germany and the Soviet Union. He pathologically feared capture. So, in the forests of what is now Ukraine,

Witkacy committed suicide during the early hours of September 18, 1939, overdosing on barbiturates and cutting his wrists.

And there matters remained for many years. But in 1956, after Khrushchev's repudiation of Stalin, things began to change. Social realism was no longer the only prescribed style of artistic expression. Witkacy's idiosyncratic and vivid plays were now enthusiastically embraced by Polish artists and intellectuals seeking to reclaim their national identity. The bibliographic climax of this resurgence was the 1962 publication of a two-volume edition with twenty plays, of which thirteen appeared for the first time.

In London, this did not go unnoticed by Stefan and Franciszka Themerson, the Polish-born publishers of Gaberbocchus Press. In the 1930s, as avant-garde filmmakers in Poland, they were aware of Witkacy's work. Stefan Themerson also shared keen interests in photography and philosophy with Witkacy. After the Second World War, the Themersons launched their small press venture and put out some sixty titles, including the first editions in English of Alfred Jarry, Guillaume Apollinaire, and Raymond Queneau, plus works by Bertrand Russell, Kurt Schwitters, Raoul Hausmann, Anatol Stern, and Stefan Themerson. Gaberbocchus was renowned for bringing important but otherwise unavailable authors to readers. Witkacy should have been perfect.

In 1967, Stefan Themerson asked Celina Wieniewska and Patrick Fetherston to collaborate on the translation and preparation of two plays by Witkacy. Wieniewska translated *Vahazar, or On the Uplands of Absurdity* (1921) and *Mother, a Tasteless Play in Two Acts with an Epilogue* (1924). She previously had made memorable translations of two Bruno Schulz collections, *The Street of Crocodiles* and *Sanatorium under the Sign of the Hourglass.* Perhaps the inclusion of *Mother* within a collection of six Witkacy plays published by University of Washington Press in 1967 caused her translation of that play to be set aside. In any case, only *Vahazar* was announced as a forthcoming title in British trade publications.

Wieniewska's translation of *Vahazar*

received a lot of attention from Gaberbocchus. Fetherston, a long-standing collaborator of the Themersons, who published two of his books of poems, was credited with adapting the translation. By comparing his adaption with a later translation of the play by Daniel Gerould, it is apparent how much Fetherston "streamlined" setting descriptions, dialogue, and stage directions. Franciszka Themerson and Barbara Wright, who translated several French authors for Gaberbocchus, also checked and revised the translation. Thus the final translation as developed by Gaberbocchus, inexplicably unseen until this publication by Black Scat Books, also might be considered an artistic version of the play.

The epilogue of this chronicle of Witkacy occurred in 1988 when the Polish government decided to give him a state funeral in Zakopane. Shortly after Ukrainian authorities produced his purported remains, it was apparent something was amiss. An X-ray of the skull was inconsistent with Witkacy's dental history. Nevertheless, the speeches, exhibitions, concerts, and entombment preceded as planned. Only later it came out the skeleton was that of a young female. So Witkacy had evaded capture again.

Paul Rosheim
July 2015

VAHAZAR

OR

ON THE UPLANDS OF ABSURDITY

CHARACTERS

Vahazar	Looks about 40. Long black moustache, disheveled hair. Foams at the mouth when furious (author's note: easy to provoke foaming by filling one's mouth with Piperazine pills). Green wide pants, dark violet boots and crimson jerkin. Black hat. Hoarse voice.
Swinella Macabescu called Swinny	A ten-year old girl, blond, dressed in white with pink ribbons. Huge black eyes. Lovely like an angel.
Donna Scabrosa Macabrescu	Swinny's mother. Age 26. A very beautiful blonde. Angelic looking.
Donna Lubrica Terramon	Donna Scabrosa's best friend. Red hair. Age 23.
Sweetoslav Terramon called Sweety	Donna Lubrica's eight year old son. Mostly silent.
Quiboozda	A miller. Age 50. Bulky, clean-shaven, with a pink face.
Doctor Ripmann	A medico. Tall and skinny. Moustache "en brosse."
Fletrick Brazemont	A writer. Age 38. Short and thin. Long hair.

Father Unguente	Age 92. Thundermitre Superior of the dissenting sect of Verticalists. Grey hair. Long black cassock. Tall pointed hat with two black wings.
Father Punguente	Age 54. Dundermitre of the dissenting order of Horizontalists. He is the younger brother of Father Unguente. Black beard down to his knees and enormous growth of black hair down to his waist. Brown cassock with yellow spots.
Four Verticalists	Dressed like Father Unguente, only without wings on hats.
Two Horizontalists	Dressed like Father Punguente, only without yellow spots on their cassocks.
Six Members of Vahazar's Guard	English type of uniforms. Black hats blue plumes.
Baron Oscar von den Binden-Gnumben	Commander of Vahazar's Guard. Age 30. Clean shaven. Uniform as others, but with red stripes and gold epaulettes.
Four Executioners:	
First	– short white moustache
Second and Third	– long black beards
Fourth: Morbidetto	– A youngster with a cruel, effeminate face. Green eyes. Red hair. All four executioners wear full body tights, short black miniskirts and red wide-brimmed hats "en bataille" with black plumes.

Crowd of petitioners Amongst others:
A Gentleman in a top hat
Second gentleman in a top hat
Dandy
First lady
Second lady
Lady of Fashion
First simple woman
Second simple woman
Workman
etc.

Author's note: Basic colours in the décor and costumes are to be pale (lemon) yellow, orangy-red, and black.

ACT 1

Waiting room adjoining the Audience Chamber in Vahazar's palace. Doors in the centre and left. Black walls. No windows. Red pattern on walls: a continuous line of irregular zig-zags, every turn ending with a yellow flame design. Two yellow columns with red spiral stripes. In the corner near left door a small table with an enormous royal-blue soda-syphon and a glass. On the centre wall a huge military coat, crimson with gold braid, hangs on a hook. No chairs, along the left wall an enormous bookcase. On the back wall a large, cubist portrait of Vahazar. On the floor black carpet with red centre and a yellow radial star. One top lamp and two lamps on the columns (directing light on each other). Door on the left padded and covered in red velvet. Over the door a stuffed large bird with a blue chain hanging from his beak.

On stage a crowd of petitioners. In the crowd: Donna Scabrosa with Swinny, Donna Lubrica with Sweety, Fletrick Brazemont, gentlemen, ladies, women etc. Scabrosa in pale-blue dress, Lubrica in green, Fletrick wears the beret, mackintosh and white gloves, Swinny in white with pink ribbons, Sweety in blue. All talk very low, then get more and more agitated, some start shouting.

FIRST GENTLEMAN
(looking at his watch)
Three o'clock in the morning! I propose that we simply depart.

LADY OF FASHION
This is truly unbearable! I've been standing here for six hours.

FIRST WOMAN
The purpose of it is, of course, to make all appraisal of reality valueless. It's all right with me.

SECOND GENTLEMAN
Oh, *please*! Do not mention the appraisal of reality in my presence.

FIRST LADY

We've been left without any criteria for it anyway.

SECOND WOMAN

All criteria are simply ir-re-le-vant!

DANDY

What?

(rubbing his knees)

Oh! My knees ache.

SWINNY

Rub in some wintergreen, Sir.

SCABROSA

Hush, child! the staying power of that girl drives me to despair.

SECOND LADY

(on her knees, facing the door leading to the Audience Chamber)

HE IS THERE! Behind that door! VA-HA-ZAR! The only ruler of all the elements and of far extending fields of general gravitation.

SECOND WOMAN

What a silly talk! Does she think nobody here is acquainted with Einstein's Theory? Nowadays, when the merest babes babble blissfully about the differential calculus?

FIRST WOMAN

Long live Gauss! Up with general coordinates. We *all* know *all* about tensors.

SECOND LADY

(prostrating herself before door)

I'd like to die waiting! I believe I'm falling at infinite speed into the abyss of absolute certainty!

FIRST GENTLEMAN

I've had enough. Let's all go to his study and tell him that we shall endure this treatment no longer.

LADY OF FASHION

Yes. Let's! Let's!

(Goes to door. SECOND LADY seizes her by the leg, laughing hysterically)

SECOND LADY

Don't go in there! Listen! Our Idol, our cruel darling!

(All listen. From behind door we hear thunderous rumbling and the moaning of a man)

FIRST GENTLEMAN

Aha! The brute! It sickens me! . . .

FLETRICK

(approaching)

How long has your Highness been waiting?

FIRST GENTLEMAN

Five hours! It's unheard of!

(crumples application form and throws it on the floor)

FLETRICK

(laughs)

Ha ha! His Highness thinks he's been waiting. Does His Highness know how long *I've* been here? Three months. Three! Six hours a day! I applied for permission to put on my play.

SECOND LADY

(all the time on her knees, shouting the loudest)

I wait and wait till I bulge out all round! O to protrude! to protrude! And all from waiting, waiting, this heavenly waiting!

(she sobs)

(BINDEN-GNUMBEN enters, eyeing everyone suspiciously)

FIRST GENTLEMAN

Captain! There's a lady here who's gone mad from waiting. This is not as it should be.

BINDEN-GNUMBEN

Silence!

(Everyone makes way for BINDEN-GNUMBEN. FIRST GENTLEMAN picks up his application form from the floor and tries to straighten it out, swearing under his breath)

SECOND LADY

(pointing to the uniform hanging on the wall)

Look: there's the symbol of his dominion. The pure embodiment of his omnipotence, all ready to envelop his delightfully developed body!

FIRST GENTLEMAN

O bloody fucking damnation! O pox and clap! God's teeth! I can't stand it any longer…

FLETRICK

Calm yourself. Your Highness, look at me. I'm not at all upset, for I look upon what's happening as part of a fictitious work. Which perhaps I might have written. Ha! Ha!

FIRST WOMAN

Quite. Life has become like a "penny dreadful".

(The door of VAHAZAR's study opens. QUIBOOZDA hurtles out, falls down prostrate beside SCABROSA, who shies away, shuddering. Everyone is rigid with fear. The two gentlemen take off their top hats)

SECOND LADY

It is HE! Our god of infinite delay! Come! Let the sacrificial suffering be mine!

VAHAZAR

(Rushes in. He howls)

Haaaaaaaaaa!!

(He halts, puts his hands in his trouserpockets, points his chin at SECOND LADY)

Throw away these old bones!

(SECOND GENTLEMAN and DANDY say nothing but drag SECOND LADY from the room)

VAHAZAR

Just so!

(to FIRST GENTLEMAN)

You first!

FIRST GENTLEMAN

(abject)

Après vous. Please!

(VAHAZAR seizes him by the scruff of the neck and pushes him through the door, follows him and bangs door behind him. A moment of silence)

SECOND GENTLEMAN

(returning)

They took her to the madhouse.

DANDY

(following him)

How mortifying! The waiting must have gone to her head.

(VAHAZAR's curses are heard from behind the door)

FLETRICK

You'd be surprised, but if you catch him at the right moment you can do what you like with him. Brutality *and* familiarity – in combination – that's the answer. Elementary psychology.

QUIBOOZDA

I must try that.

(RIPMANN enters)

RIPMANN

Everyone's papers in order?

ALL

Yes! Yes! Papers in order! All of them!

RIPMANN

Not so loud! I'm very anxious about the state of His Superiority's heart. His pulse is 146 a minute. Kindly do not irritate him, or I shall have to cancel the audiences for today.

LADY OF FASHION

O God! I've been waiting for seven hours. My feet have gone to sleep.

(sits on floor)

RIPMANN

Oh! Be serious. There are people here who've been waiting for months.

(Another roar from VAHAZAR is heard)

FIRST WOMAN

That uncanny, erotic quality of his voice…

RIPMANN

His strength is superhuman.

(pause)

It's something I don't understand.

FLETRICK

Drugs?

RIPMANN

Nothing of the kind. His Radiance is a total abstainer. Besides, he sleeps only one hour a night and works like sixty diesel-driven dinosaurs. – I still haven't been able to bring round the ambassador of Illyria after this morning's conference. But they've worked out a new programme for the upbringing of little girls. A masterpiece! Superb!

SCABROSA

That's of particular interest to *me*. Could you give me some details, doctor?

SWINNY

To me too. I want to be a lady-in-waiting at the Court of His Fabulosity. And I want a red visiting card with all that printed on it.

RIPMANN

(to SCABROSA)

No difficulty at all. The results will be miraculous.

(Door opens, VAHAZAR enters, shouting)

VAHAZAR

You friggomite! You acne-ridden crooklouse! You dare to come here with a crumpled application form! – and you dare to sign yourself Prince! You perforated sissigrampus! You flopsack! Listen now! All of you! I've always said you were all equal before me. You are nothing. You are absolutely nothing! I abandon myself to total solitude – and it's all for *you*! Nobody's my equal. Understand? My brain's as big as a vat of beer. I could have become whatever I wanted to be. You understand? Eh?

FLETRICK

(shaking voice)

I feel…that up to a point…I'm beginning to understand…a little.

VAHAZAR

I'll give you 'up to a point'. You want to die 'up to a point', you sloughy snake!

FLETRICK

(overcome with terror)

Nothing. I…er… Your extremity.

VAHAZAR

Shut up and listen! You have *some* intelligence, don't you? I sacrifice myself for *you*. None of you can appreciate that. But I don't expect appreciation. I know you spread a lot of filthy gossip about me. I'm alone. Like God. I govern myself. I'm answerable to nobody but myself for what I do. I may even sentence myself to death, if the whim takes me. My civil servants are like automatons – you know, slotmachines, the things they have in railway stations. I insert a coin and out comes a chocolate – and not a mint humbug. Chocolate! You understand now?

FLETRICK

Yes; now I...understand completely, for the first time...

VAHAZAR

(interrupting)

Good. And now shut up.

(changing his tone)

I'm leading you all to unimaginable happiness. Each one of you will dwell in his own little box lined with cotton-wool, like a priceless jewel, alone, unique in the superhuman dignity of his deepest being – just as I am now. But *I* suffer, like all the souls in hell, for *your* sake. I'm as pure as a lonely maiden thinking of the white flowers of her metaphysical piety. I am myself such a flower, risen from the dark centre of an omnipresent whole. I'm lonely as a pearl inside an oyster in the depths of . . .

(FLETRICK, who for some time has tried to contain himself, roars with laughter, and is overcome by hysterical cramp)

VAHAZAR

All right: laugh. I know I can't speak your literary lingo. You're all free to laugh – to say anything to my face. But none of you will dare to do so – because it means death. This is what freedom means. I tell you: new people can only be created through destruction and not by filling their heads with pretty thoughts – as Mr Fletrick, or whatever his name is, does. Well, let him play. And I shall destroy – in the name of resplendent little flowers which will blossom in the souls of your children who, at the instant of awakening in the desert of the spirit, will howl for one drop of that something – that mighty something which is so tiny that it may be glimpsed inside each little worm, each blade of grass, each fragment of crystal buried in rock . . .

FLETRICK

(interrupting)

Is it to be found in the bedbug, which bites you in the night, Your Metaphysical Nonentity?

VAHAZAR

(coldly, in a quivering voice)

What?

FLETRICK

(brutally)

I asked you if you could find this something in a bedbug, you old buffoon.

(VAHAZAR whistles for his guards. Six guards and BINDEN-GNUMBEN enter)

VAHAZAR

Shoot that clown!

(They remove FLETRICK, who is quite limp and rather surprised)

VAHAZAR

As I said, I want to give you that little something, even if you have to go through inconceivable suffering first . . .

FIRST WOMAN

That's all very well, Your Consequence, but what is that something?

VAHAZAR

I could know it if I wanted to, my dear. But I don't. If I did, I'd no longer be the man of action I am. You understand?

(A volley of shots is heard)

VAHAZAR

One scribbler the less. I don't like writing myself and I can't bear graphomaniacs. Foh! Those dirty dogs.

OLD WORKER

(in crowd)

All right, all right. You've promised all this for our grandchildren. But what about *us*? What do *we* get out of it?

VAHAZAR

Nothing. We have to transcend our egotism – otherwise we shan't create anything.

FIRST WOMAN

Yes, but Your Luxuriance has lived well and we . . .

SCABROSA

Certainly. He's lived well. No question of that!

VAHAZAR

Please don't interrupt.

(to FIRST WOMAN)

Do you think you count – as an individual? Of course you don't. Even *I* don't. I suffer more than any of you. Rejoice that you suffer at the side of such a man as I! I wish you wouldn't drive me into empty rhetoric. And – in particular – don't force me to *think*. Because, if I wanted to, I could think it all out, overnight – and tomorrow morning I could rise a different man, and be incapable of doing anything at all. You complain that you've been waiting so long with your petitions. The Jews have also been waiting.

For the Messiah. And they produced Cantor, Husserl and Bergson – I hate that humbug though – Marx, and Einstein. Don't think I like Jews, but it's a fact.

FIRST WOMAN

Just so: the Jews had waited. And when the Messiah came, they killed him.

VAHAZAR

Woman! Don't take advantage of my patience! Be thankful that you're *waiting for* something.

(He laughs)

You probably think I talk too much, using up the time in which I could be dealing with your petitions . . . All right.

(to OLD WORKER, taking his petition)

You first.

RIPMANN

(meanwhile taking VAHAZAR's pulse)

Your Supremacy! . . .175 . . . Not a moment more. Finish!

(QUIBOOZDA hurries in, carrying a bottle of wine)

QUIBOOZDA

You! Vahazar! Come here at once! I mean business!

(Gives him a poke in the ribs; thrusts out petition)

Either you read it, you bastard, or I'll knock your block off!

FIRST WOMAN

(admiringly)

And to think that no one dares to kill him!

VAHAZAR

Ha ha, you see, my dear? I've got a special inner fluid.

(VAHAZAR tears up the petition. QUIBOOZDA loses momentum somewhat, but tries again, hitting VAHAZAR on the head heavily)

QUIBOOZDA

Will you answer me, you twerp? My mill's got to start working again. I've no time for your nonsense . . .

VAHAZAR

(as if waking from a dream)

What is it?

QUIBOOZDA

The mill! Sign this! You poxy devil! And we'll drink to it!

VAHAZAR

(abstracted)

That's interesting, yes . . .

QUIBOOZDA

(at the height of his fury)

Sign, you sod!

VAHAZAR

What will that do?

QUIBOOZDA

(slightly taken aback)

Nothing . . . The mill will turn again. Don't try pulling my leg, short-arse, or I'll break your neck!

VAHAZAR

I'm somewhat reluctant . . .

(He signs QUIBOOZDA's paper)

By the way, I don't drink.

(Shakes QUIBOOZDA by the hand.

QUIBOOZDA goes out, holding his head)

RIPMANN

Your Magnificence: not one single application more! It could kill you.

(confidentially)

There is just a certain lady I'd like you to see. Her daughter wishes to be a New Model Lady-in-Waiting.

(to SCABROSA)

Please. Come over here.

(The others slowly leave. SCABROSA with SWINNY, LUBRICA with SWEETY, remain)

SCABROSA

(approaching VAHAZAR)

Don't you remember me, Uncle?

VAHAZAR

(vaguely)

No . . .

SCABROSA

You brought me up! And then, that day . . . or was it night?

VAHAZAR

Perhaps, perhaps. But that's immaterial. I've wiped out all traces of my past.

RIPMANN

Any reminders of the past have a bad effect on the health of His Presence.

SCABROSA

Never mind then. The fact is my daughter's determined to become a lady-in-waiting at your court. Come, Swinny! Wish Grandpa a good morning.

VAHAZAR

Come, little one! I'm delighted to find that you're so far-seeing.

SWINNY

But I don't want to wait – like all those people. I want everything at once!

VAHAZAR

Yes, you'll have it all at once!

(to SCABROSA)

Sweet angel, I shall do whatever I can for her. The programme is to develop ladies-in-waiting into perfect specimens of mechanical motherhood.

(To SWINNY, giving her some sweets from his pocket)

Here are some sweets, darling.

(Bends down)

What intelligent eyes you have, my little pigeon!

RIPMANN

(anxiously)

Your Unbendability, perhaps you're feeling faint . . . A glass of water?

VAHAZAR

So you think I'm getting soft in the head. Eh? On the contrary, I feel fine. Well, you can give me some water if you want to.

(to SCABROSA)

And you, madam. Will you agree to total separation? We've just today been putting the finishing touches to the syllabus for the upbringing of little girls. A wonderful programme! Paragraph one: to hell with all their mamas!

(RIPMANN brings water. VAHAZAR drinks)

I can't stand ordinary women anywhere near me. I should really like to mechanize them all. We divide women into real females, whom we mechanize out of hand, and femaloons, whom we turn into men by grafting the relevant glands . . . Am I right, Mr. Ripmann?

RIPMANN

Right, Your Righteousness.

(to SCABROSA)

We'll have unbelievable results.

SCABROSA

But, Your Serenity, I should like to be as I am. Perhaps a little happier . . .

VAHAZAR

There's nothing to discuss. You look like a femaloon to me. Your eyes are too clever.

LUBRICA

(approaching them)

Your Magistracy, she's my friend.

VAHAZAR

What! You here too? You, who've been

pestering me with your love . . . ? Here's a shrewd girl – I'm glad you've turned up. We can make an excellent civil servant of her. Eh, Mr. Ripmann?

RIPMANN

Yes, Your Sagacity. She's certainly no specimen of mechanical motherhood!

VAHAZAR

Well, Dr. Ripmann, I think you might arrange for these ladies to be sent to the Sexual Qualities Control Commission.

LUBRICA

(hysterically)

Vahazar! Beware of tampering with the species! Or it will take its revenge. You'll create a society in which the mechanized females will devour their mates just as some insects do. You will be drones, and we'll slaughter you when you're no longer needed.

VAHAZAR

Ha ha ha! Doesn't she talk well, Dr. Ripmann? What a mind! She'll be a perfect official.

SCABROSA

What about my Swinny? What will become of her?

VAHAZAR

This will be determined by the Commission for Supernatural Selection after a fortnight of preliminary training. This is how I translate my personal suffering into cosmic values. I'm the first martyr of the sixth-dimensional continuum . . . and I'm entirely alone . . .

SWINNY

Grandpapa, that can't be true. There is someone behind you who's whispering in your ear.

VAHAZAR

(disconcerted)

Nonsense! You must have heard some gossip . . .

SWINNY

It's *not* nonsense, Grandpapa. He's right here.

VAHAZAR

(looking at his watch)

It's nearly four o'clock. I have to go.

SWINNY

Don't escape! Look me in the eyes.

(They are very close together)

I can see right down into you, down to the bottom, where horrible red worms with black heads crawl about . . . I see still further . . . What is all your suffering for, Grandpapa? *Stop* suffering.

VAHAZAR

My inner fluid isn't working. Dr. Ripmann! I feel faint! Help!

(RIPMANN takes his pulse)

RIPMANN

To bed, to bed immediately. Your Faintness. There's no pulse at all.

(to the women)

This is a sort of internal narcosis . . . It must be the poison from some unknown gland. I've always said, and I repeat, that the gland is the essence of medicine.

SWINNY

Grandpapa, you can now see what I see. Think for a moment – and then you'll understand.

VAHAZAR

Swinny, don't talk like that. An extra-ordinary world of quiet, exquisite beauty opens out before me . . . Dr. Ripmann! Water!

(He staggers)

It's nothing. It must be glands.

SWINNY

Not glands at all! It's *he* – the one beside you – it's yourself. You're coiled round yourself like a snake.

(pause)

Now you see a green meadow. And a little kennel. In the little kennel sits a little dog with a red ribbon. I see that every night before I go to sleep.

(VAHAZAR looks at her as if hypnotized)

RIPMANN

To bed, Your Invincibility!

(Four EXECUTIONERS, including MORBIDETTO, come in)

SWEETY

Good morning, gentlemen. I belong to the

male section.

(The women look around, then scream with fright at the sight of the EXECUTIONERS. They cover their eyes and remain motionless. MORBIDETTO quietly, with a leer, approaches VAHAZAR, looks into his face. Suddenly VAHAZAR shudders and wakes up)

VAHAZAR

Haaaaaaaaa! First: those two females. They're to go to the Sexual Qualities Control Commission! Shoot all the old tabbies in District Four: withdraw all permits for special marriages! Call all pedagogues to an Extraordinary General Meeting. Haaaaaaa!

RIPMANN

To bed, to bed, Your Inevitability!

(MORBIDETTO takes VAHAZAR's arm and leads him slowly out)

VAHAZAR

(going)

Thank you, my dear Morbidetto. I had a moment of weakness . . .

(Exit, followed by three of the EXECUTIONERS. RIPMANN takes SWINNY by the hand)

RIPMANN

And you, my dear, will go to our Court Boarding School.

(SCABROSA stretches out her arms towards SWINNY)

SWINNY

I'll be all right, Mama. I'm not afraid of his roars. Nothing can happen to me.

(RIPMANN leads her out)

SWEETY

What fun! I'm in the male section, so it's none of my business really, any of this . . .

(LUBRICA embraces SWEETY. SCABROSA quietly weeps)

BINDEN-GRUMBEN

(entering; coolly)

Ladies, would you kindly follow me?

CURTAIN

ACT 2

Red Audience Chamber in Vahazar's palace. The walls are red and so is the carpet, which has in the middle a yellow star with a black center. Lemon-yellow furniture in fantastic shapes – e.g. wings rising from the backs of the chairs – black fantastic patterns on the wooden parts. In the centre a window, through which a landscape of rolling green hills can be seen. In the distance: the City with towers and smoking chimneys.

LUBRICA

(holding a huge black envelope covered with seals)

O God! What's to become of us? The shameful treatment from that commission!

SCABROSA

(totally apathetic; with a similar envelope in her hand)

And now another stretch of waiting, till we go mad! Our whole life is in those envelopes.

The least they could have done was to tell us straight away.

LUBRICA

Brutes! – When I was a little girl I always wanted to be a boy – and now the thought of it makes me sick.

SCABROSA

You, at any rate, have your Sweetie. And there's no programme for boys yet. I'm quite alone. Even my poor Swinny has been torn from me. I don't care. I wouldn't even mind being a femaloon, as long as she could be happy.

(Pause. A maid comes in with SWINNY, who carries a huge doll resembling VAHAZAR)

SWINNY

Mama! Mama! Look! Isn't Grandpapa Vahazar lovely? I can just guess what he's thinking when I pull his moustache.

(She runs to SCABROSA and lays her doll on her lap. SCABROSA weeps)

SWINNY

Why are you crying, Mama? *I'm* not frightened.

SCABROSA

But I shan't be seeing you till you're grown up.

SWINNY

Mama! You should be ashamed to cry like that. I slept beautifully. They gave me chocolate and cakes for breakfast. And pink pussies are painted on the bathtub.

(SCABROSA gets up, letting the VAHAZAR doll fall to the floor; laughs through her tears)

SCABROSA

Ha ha ha! Pink pussies on a bathtub! Perhaps he's got one like that as well – that bastard! that rabid clown!

(She laughs hysterically)

(SWINNY dances with the doll round and round the room. RIPMANN, in a white overall, comes in)

RIPMANN

Good morning, good morning. Have you been to the commission?

(SCABROSA and LUBRICA run up to him)

SCABROSA/LUBRICA

Yes, yes. Please, doctor, tell us the result. Would you open the envelopes?

RIPMANN

I'm not authorized to open them. That is the privilege of His Authority Vahazar the First.

LUBRICA

Could he but be the last?

RIPMANN

(severely)

Your limited intelligence cannot grasp the immensity of this genius' mind. This is *Re-a-li-ty* with a capital R.

LUBRICA

Ugh! Clichés with a capital C. I'm amazed that a man as shrewd as you can be taken in . . .

RIPMANN

You're looking through a small magnifying glass at things that really demand the biggest telescopes and a distance of a thousand light-years. One shouldn't listen to his words but scrutinize his deeds. I could point to an analogy with the disintegration of psychic atoms and, as radium goes through multifarious transformations, throwing off tremendous energy, he, similarly, will be transformed into a different man. He *will*, or I'll say all my medicine is bosh.

LUBRICA

Bosh or not bosh as it may be. It's all very well; you live here in comfort and have a wonderful psychiatric laboratory with the most interesting madman in the whole world. If only we could kill him.

RIPMANN

One would have to be a superlunatic to do so. The people know he leads them where nobody else can lead them. They know by instinct that he tortures them and suffers for them all at the same time. The same tendencies are in evidence in many different countries.

LUBRICA

It will all end up in a general crumple such as the world has never seen.

(Door opens. VAHAZAR enters)

VAHAZAR

Any documents for me?

(SCABROSA and LUBRICA run to him, with their envelopes)

RIPMANN

(to the women)

You should thank His Uniqueness that you didn't have to wait. Sometimes it takes months.

VAHAZAR

(under his breath)

Yes, yes, and it's not my fault. I've no time. You force me into this position. And if anyone dares to force me, he must take the consequences.

SCABROSA/LUBRICA

What's in the letters, Your Gracefulness?

(VAHAZAR, impatient, puts the letters into his pocket)

VAHAZAR

Dr. Ripmann: those women in District Four . . . Have they been shot, as I ordered?

RIPMANN

They have, Your Felicity. All the officers rebelled. They've been imprisoned.

VAHAZAR

Good. Hang all of them, except one. You know, that short little one in the Seventh Regiment.

RIPMANN

Yes, Your Sodomy.

VAHAZAR

We'll have chocolate cream for lunch. – Swinny likes chocolate.

(To MAID)

Miss Swinny's evening dress has to be ready for seven o'clock.

MAID

Yes, Your Benevolence.

SCABROSA

Just a minute. Your Benignity! What's in those papers.

VAHAZAR

(to SCABROSA)

Don't be so pertinacious. – Dr. Ripmann, I don't want to talk to anybody today till two o'clock. I've just heard from the Albanian Ambassador that someone's been impersonating me out there.

(Laughs uncontrollably. SWINNY laughs too)

SWINNY

Grandpapa! Dance with me!

(For a moment they dance around the stage. RIPMANN with a fatherly smile. Suddenly holds up his hand)

RIPMANN

Enough, Your Incredibility! Remember your pulse!

VAHAZAR

O yes. My pulse . . .

(seizes hold of his own wrist)

O nothing . . . no more than 150.

SWINNY

Grandpapa! May I pull your moustache?

VAHAZAR

Certainly! Pull away! You can play with me as if I were a doll.

SWINNY

Look me in the eyes, Grandpapa. Why do you turn away?

(VAHAZAR shuts his eyes. Silence. He opens his eyes)

SWINNY

I see your soul, a little worn-out soul. It's blue and it wanders among the stalks of grass, stroking little beetles.

(VAHAZAR, in a daze, sits on the floor in front of her)

VAHAZAR

You drive away my loneliness. I'm not alone when I'm with you. I see quite a different world. A glade in the forest. And I see you

with a big dog and some young man . . .
Good heavens, it's me!

SWINNY

(She strokes his hair. VAHAZAR covers his eyes)

Walk a little further; and don't look away.

VAHAZAR

Yes, it is I. I! I! It's been such a long time since I saw the green grass and the trees. I see the butterflies. They're chasing each other. Swinny, lead me along. I'll do anything you wish.

LUBRICA

Ask him to tell us what's in those envelopes.

(VAHAZAR wakes up)

SWINNY

You've spoilt everything now! Like a naughty child.

(She clasps her hands)

VAHAZAR

Haaaaaa! Now I'm rested. I've been resting for centuries. Now I have to work. I need the strength of sixty electrified bulls. I want to bend everything. I want to squash it into a pulp. To work, to work, Dr. Ripmann!

SCABROSA

The papers!

VAHAZAR

You'll find everything out in good time, my little turtledoves. You can wait. Now let's get that Albanian here, the one who's been taking me off. Haaaaaaaaa!

(The door opens. Four VERTICALISTS carry FATHER UNGUENTE in on a stretcher)

FATHER UNGUENTE

(in a quiet penetrating voice)

I'm not afraid of your roaring, Vahazar. You were my pupil. I don't know how many times I gave you bad marks for differential calculus; how many times you were kept after lessons.

VAHAZAR

(standing momentarily speechless)

It's you, Professor, sir.

(Voice of a frightened pupil)

FATHER UNGUENTE

I'm no longer a professor. I'm a high priest of the new religion. Today we emerged from underground. I have over 20,000 followers. In that subterranean darkness I begot a new world of truth, the terror of all liars.

VAHAZAR

(as before)

I'm not a liar. It's *they* who force me to carry on like that. And I never lie.

FATHER UNGUENTE

Nobody's accused you of lying. I believe that you're truthful. But without faith you'll create nothing, silly boy. You're in darkness like every living thing, from the smallest worm up to myself, who knows only what a finite and limited creature can know.

VAHAZAR

So you *know*? You don't *believe*?

FATHER UNGUENTE

The highest knowledge and the highest faith converge, because they both uncover the depths of the same mystery. Look at me. I have gout and I suffer. And I don't care about my pain, which is boundless. Owwwww! Put me on the floor, you bleeding Verticalists. I'm only a heap of agonized bones, but I created something without which your work, Vahazar, is little better than the convulsions of a madman. *You have to come over to my side*!

VAHAZAR

(coolly and mechanically)

He who forces me must answer for the consequences.

FATHER UNGUENTE

Don't worry. I *will*. You must join me because without the faith based on ultimate knowledge you'll be just like a figure in a comic strip: like Alexander the Great, Peter the Great – Vahazar the Great, in reality pathetic little lunatics. A tiny fish lost in the net of metaphysical contradiction.

SWINNY

I told you nearly the same thing, Grandpapa.

(FATHER UNGUENTE turns to her)

VAHAZAR

Wait, Swinny.

(To FATHER UNGUENTE)

I know all that tomfoolery. Ho ho! Professor! Philosophy and life both in love with the same chap. They're irreconcilable.

FATHER UNGUENTE

(with distaste)

Not philosophy. Real knowledge! Through knowledge we should come to faith, not through theosophical humbug created for mediocrities and misfits. Submit yourself, you caricature of Cæsar and all the other megalomaniacs! I've been reading a squib about you that they've distributed in District Four: 'The devil calls me Cancer of the Navel and the old gods call me Infinity's Own Louse'. That's what it said.

VAHAZAR

What!?

FATHER UNGUENTE

On your knees, Vahazar! *That's* what.

(VAHAZAR kneels. FATHER PUNGUENTE comes in with two HORIZONTALISTS)

FATHER PUNGUENTE

I beg your pardon . . . I didn't mean to interrupt . . . I'm chief Dundermitre of the barefoot Horizontalists. I've just learnt that my brother has achieved his object. We've come to do homage. May we?

VAHAZAR

(getting up)

O do! by all means! We were only rehearsing a scene from a play about Henry the Fourth and Pope Gregory the Seventh. We've finished now.

(FATHER PUNGUENTE and the HORIZONTALISTS kneel before FATHER UNGUENTE)

FATHER PUGUENTE

We are all heretics and sectarians, and religion is finished. Nevertheless, I shall kneel before my dear brother.

(Kneels before FATHER UNGUENTE. All the HORIZONTALISTS also kneel before him. The VERTICALISTS stand erect)

FATHER UNGUENTE

You do well to kneel before me, but I don't really mind heresies, and any new sect is new evidence of the Church's vitality. I allow every possible heresy.

FATHER PUNGUENTE

Brother, you've made me so happy! I shall start a new sect this afternoon!

SWINNY

(running up to FATHER UNGUENTE)

I shall start a new little church myself. I saw it in a dream.

(VAHAZAR, taken aback, looks up in surprise)

FATHER UNGUENTE

I bless you, my child. You have a great future.

(SWINNY kneels before FATHER UNGUENTE)

VAHAZAR

(roaring and throwing himself on FATHER UNGUENTE)

Haaaaaa! You animated gangrene! I'll show

you what a pain in the bones is really like. *Now* d'know what absolute knowledge is? *Now* d'know how to make faith out of it?

(The VERTICALISTS drag VAHAZAR away from FATHER UNGUENTE, who lies in a dead faint on his stretcher. The women crowd round him and try to revive him. SWINNY stands on one side, smiling. The HORIZONTALISTS, with FATHER PUNGUENTE, gather together in the corner)

VAHAZAR
(still held by the VERTICALISTS)
Dr. Ripmann, I made a fool of myself . . .

RIPMANN
I'd put it down to overwork.

VAHAZAR
Order them let go of me! I'm as weak as… a child.

(SWINNY goes to armchair, takes up the VAHAZAR doll and plays with it)

RIPMANN

(to the VERTICALISTS)

Do let go of His Foolishness.

VAHAZAR

How unhappy I am! No one understands me. I need warmth, a little tenderness, a pinch of love!

(cries quickly)

LUBRICA

Vahazar! I always – ! I'm beside you!

SWEETY

(without rising from seat at back)

Mama! Mama! Leave him alone. I know I belong to the male section, and it's not my business, but I can't allow *this*!

VAHAZAR

It's not what I want, anyway! I want a mother; or at least a sister!

LUBRICA

Well, that's what I wanted to be for you, believe me. I didn't want anything from you. I simply wanted you to visit me, sometimes, and have a cup of tea with me.

VAHAZAR
(shivers)
Ugh! I'm exhausted!

SWINNY
Aunt Lubrica! Leave him alone! He's so pitiful.

SCABROSA
(irritated, to SWINNY)
You don't understand a thing, you stupid child! I've begun to think you're not quite normal. Don't interfere!

(Four EXECUTIONERS, among them MORBIDETTO, enter and stand, unnoticed, against the wall)

SWINNY
Oh! Do let him alone!

VAHAZAR
(irritated, to SWINNY)
Don't you see it's useless? She doesn't understand.
(Very stiffly to LUBRICA and SCABROSA)
I shall now read your papers.
(Takes them out of his pocket)

Donna Scabrosa Makabrescu: 30% woman; 65% femaloon; 5% psychical oddments. Fine.

(He goes on reading)

Donna Lubrica Terramon: 43% woman; 55% femaloon; 2% oddments. – Perfect. Dr. Ripmann: would you take care of these ladies? Why are the chances of a real mechanical mother so remote these days?

(FATHER UNGUENTE wakes up groaning)

VAHAZAR

(noticing MORBIDETTO)

O it's you, my only friend! Save me! I need somebody to put his cool hand on my hot forehead . . .

(MORBIDETTO suddenly throws himself between VAHAZAR and the women like a darting snake)

MORBIDETTO

You dare to feel that way! *You*! I shall kill you.

(Very high, squeaking voice for the last word)

SCABROSA

(pointing at MORBIDETTO)

He's the only one with the guts to stand up to this monster.

SWINNY

O mama! Stop! It's too late!

MORBIDETTO

Yes, it *is* too late. You can be off to the clinic, both of you. Dr. Ripmann, takes these females away.

RIPMANN

I take orders from no one but His Adorability.

MORBIDETTO

I'm the only one who can kill you, Vahazar. And you know that.

VAHAZAR

(suddenly furious)

You're just like all the others! Such riffraff perpetually tagging along and besmirching my great deeds…! At least they can't pollute my ideas, as I don't formulate them. I wish to build a huge palace of porphyry, and all the material I have is this disgusting human refuse.

MORBIDETTO

You've brought all that on yourself. You've willed your own weakness. This is your last anodyne, crowning all the privations which were meant to drug you. What a monstrous come-down! And that other one, that sickening phoney magician with his 'absolute knowledge' . . . What a contradiction! And if we were ever to admit the contradiction, how could we distinguish the true from the false?

VAHAZAR

You may well be right. But how can I be sure?

SWINNY

Grandpapa, listen to me! I'll lead you out of this maze.

MORBIDETTO

(stroking her head)

Little girl, you don't understand a thing. Just run away and play with your doll.

SWINNY

(shrinking away)

I know you: you're clever because you *want*

to be clever, just like *him*.

(Points to FATHER UNGUENTE)

And Grandpapa could be clever if he wanted to; but he doesn't; and he's right. You're too clever and too silly – all at the same time.

(SWINNY resumes play with doll)

VAHAZAR

Enough of it all! Here I am! I'm just like a black star against the backdrop of a white-hot night. I'll arrest everybody! Everybody present, do you hear! To jail! – Come, Morbidetto, you've saved me from a fatal act of weakness; I shan't forget this. Now: to work, work, work! You understand, Dr. Ripmann?

RIPMANN

Yes, Your Indefatigability.

VAHAZAR

(led by MORBIDETTO)

My soul will never feel the joys of weakness now. My destiny, in this disgusting, cramped world, I am determined to fulfill . . . Hell and brimstone! Even if I have to torture everyone to death!

SWINNY

I think I love him as if he was my father.

LUBRICA

(her hand over SWINNY's mouth)

Don't say that!

FATHER UNGUENTE

Come here, my child.

(SWINNY runs to him)

You're the only one who knows the truth – even though you don't know it. You're marked for sacrifice by your sacred imbecility.

RIPMANN

Don't put ideas into the child's head, Father Unguente. The solution to everything lies in the glands. At present I'm working on mice. But when His Perspicacity finally lets me experiment on human beings, the categories of *genius* and *imbecile* in relation to the category of *man* will be like water and ice in relation to H_2O. Science is not on the way out, Father Unguente.

FATHER UNGUENTE

I never suggested science was on the way

out. But for physicists the universe is now finite and non-Euclidean, while for me it's infinite and amorphous. Real space is without structure. This is the absolute truth which uses physical truth as a comfortable analogue. D'you follow me?

RIPMANN

I propose to inject you with certain secretions from the gland of doubt, and then you won't be so sure.

(BINDEN-GNUMBEN enters with his guard)

BINDEN-GNUMBEN

Everybody's under arrest! By order of His Omniscience!

RIPMANN

(smiling)

With the exception of myself, I take it.

BINDEN-GNUMBEN

Everybody. You understand, Dr. Ripmann. I don't make mistakes. – Get up, all of you, and follow me.

SWINNY

What fun! Grandpapa's suddenly decided to make a completely new play.

(The HORIZONTALISTS carry FATHER UNGUENTE off on his stretcher, and everyone goes, RIPMANN following)

RIPMANN

Trust those glands to come up with a surprise like that!

CURTAIN

ACT 3

Cell No. 17 in the Paupers of Genius prison. Dark-brown walls and yellow columns. The air full of smoke. Straw on the floor right and left. In centre wooden steps leading upwards to an iron door which is shaken at regular intervals by somebody beating against it with a hammer from outside. The cell is lit by orange bulbs placed high on the wall. The reddish light is darkened by dense spirals of trailing smoke.

Lying around on the straw all the company, except for QUIBOOZDA, VAHAZAR and BINDEN-GNUMBEN. LUBRICA and SCABROSA in gentlemen's suits. SWINNY in red dress with yellow pattern.

LUBRICA
(to MORBIDETTO)
What now! Perhaps you'll entertain us with some witty conversation? Or perhaps you'll devise some extraordinary torments for us?

MORBIDETTO
(yawning)
They'll come in time. But I'm sure they aren't worth starting on.

LUBRICA
You know Vahazar best.

MORBIDETTO
I know him in his bouts of fury and anger, but I don't understand his moments of kindness and calm. They must be conscious deceptions.

LUBRICA
Oh?

MORBIDETTO
If he dares to put *me* in prison it means that any tender weakness is alien to him. D'you know that from this moment I've come to *believe* in his superhuman strength?

LUBRICA
What did you believe in before?

MORBIDETTO
In my complete, absolute, infinite,

metaphysical, multidimensional *Vice*!

LUBRICA

If this scoundrel got shaken, we are all doomed.

RIPMANN

That bastard! Pah! Do you forget that *I* am in prison too? I! The famous Doctor Joseph Jeremy Ripmann, Fellow of the Society of Medical Thinkers, creator of the newest formula in the theory of Glands Manipulation! Years of experiment! Exciting results!

(lecturing voice)

Let us suppose that my conception of the disintegration of atoms . . .

(with sudden despair)

Oh! how ridiculous it sounds, all that blah-blah in the face of death!

MORBIDETTO

Tut tut, Dr. Ripmann! One can't know who's the most important in the circle round Vahazar. And remember: the death penalty is for both the informer and the traitor.

RIPMANN

(immediately)

I'm neither an informer nor a traitor. I'm only a very, very modest scientist . . .

MORBIDETTO

Just like me. I am only a very, very, modest executioner. Of course, I tortured prisoners, following my orders. And if Vahazar preferred *me* to do it rather than anyone else, that's no fault of mine. I'd sooner not look into his personal inclinations in public.

SCABROSA

What! Who? Him? The monster!

MORBIDETTO

She's guessed it at last, the silly bitch.

LUBRICA

What has she guessed? Do tell!

SCABROSA

Nothing. Nothing.

MORBIDETTO

(complacent)

Perhaps I've not been imprisoned at all.

Perhaps my master put me here so that I might learn something of your attitude. Eh?

RIPMANN

(anxiously trying to reassure himself)

He could find people worthier of observation than us.

MORBIDETTO

(sly)

Aren't you being a little *too* modest?

RIPMANN

On my word of honour, no! I was a very modest scientist; my aims were purely theoretical; I lived only for my research.

MORBIDETTO

Aha! Glands! We know something about them . . . The Sexual Qualities Commission . . . and visits to District Four.

RIPMANN

(with forced gaiety)

Morbidetto, you're joking. Have you a cigarette? This is my fifth day without one.

MORBIDETTO
(reaches for a box)
Here you are. I don't smoke, but I always have this on me, just in case.

(RIPMANN takes one, lights it)

RIPMANN
Ah! What delight!

MORBIDETTO
You're an imbecile, dear doctor. You pretend to be Sherlock Holmes. I give the word of the greatest scoundrel in the country that I've been arrested entirely according to the rules. And to be arrested by His Inflexibility is worse than death; it may be tor-ture!
(Pronounces the first syllable on a high note, the second low)

RIPMANN
This sort of talk gives me gooseflesh.

MORBIDETTO
One could always kill oneself.

RIPMANN
(imploringly)
Is there no hope at all?
(Silence)
There's a hideous void inside me. *Hideous*, I tell you.

FATHER UNGUENTE
I believe you, my son. I shouldn't like to be you for one second. When I was listening to you all I wondered if it was worthwhile for sages, prophets and artists to toil for this disgusting bag of worms . . . Have you seen the prison latrine? Soup with wriggling vermicelli. You have the same effect on me, gentlemen. And this is the cream of humanity!

RIPMANN
I'm ashamed. But I'm terribly frightened – At least I'm *sincere.*

MORBIDETTO
Anyone's sincere who has nothing to lose. – Dr. Ripmann, your sincerity is fouling the air.

RIPMANN
Oh! Sorry!

FATHER UNGUENTE
Gentlemen, does it mean nothing to you that there are ladies present?

SWINNY
Let's be silent. Sh, sh, sh!

(Nobody pays any attention)

RIPMANN
Listen, Morbidetto. You came here five days after us. Tell us in detail what happened.

MORBIDETTO
Nothing. The Albanian ambassador collapsed from overwork . . . We tortured some army officers for sixteen hours. Then they put me in a Black Maria – and here I am.

RIPMANN
This is terrible!

SWINNY
No, it's *not* terrible! Illumination will come!

FATHER UNGUENTE
Listen to that girl. Through her you hear the same spirit that, in me, has been transformed

into notions.

SWINNY

There's something holy I know . . . And when I tell you what it is you'll all be like me, and we'll be reunited in infinity. Not once but an infinite number of times.

FATHER UNGUENTE

(with elation)

Go on, go on, child! Go on, voice of innocence! O great faith floating in the existential infinity! – O what a poor soul Einstein is! Lost speck of dust! Pathetic little worm!

SWINNY

You don't understand anything, Father Unguente. It's not infinity: it's this instant only, I mean . . .

(She clasps hands over her breast)

(VAHAZAR falls in, pushed through the door)

VAHAZAR

Wretches! Pseudodemocracy, autocracy, levellocracy, embodied in the nonexistence of otherworldly powers, is on the march! Everything's conquering everything. Nothing's conquering everything. And everything's conquering nothing – with a capital N. Listen to me, you metaphysical courtesans! Listen to me, you wise old men! And you, child, innocent lamb! ME-E-E! ME-E-E-E!

(He falls in a fit)

RIPMANN

Oh! Your Invincibility!

VAHAZAR

Now everything is lost; I've been jailed. Death awaits me tomorrow, along with all my followers. *You* are my followers. *You and I* will be executed together. *He* has triumphed.

LUBRICA/SCABROSA

Who? Who?

VAHAZAR

He. He! The accursed one, of whom I've always been afraid.

MORBIDETTO

I *knew* there was somebody stronger than Vahazar. I felt it in my bones. I can already picture him . . . Vahazar, tell me! Is it that one, you know . . .

VAHAZAR

(his hands over his eyes)

Yes.

RIPMANN

I knew it too! I saw him in a dream. I know his face . . . Only I can't remember it. What a torment! Not to remember!

VAHAZAR

Yes, you're both right. – O it's unbearable! I want to die. Kill me!

(Lies on the floor groaning)

MORBIDETTO

Aha, that may be the solution. Shall we betray him? Perhaps treachery will give us a new lease of life. Life from the beginning. Life without Vahazar. Who could imagine the beauty of that life?

FATHER UNGUENTE

But who can take up the heavy burden he was carrying? Whoever comes after him must be more pusillanimous.

RIPMANN
I always said the whole Vahazar business was humbug. If only I could trace the gland responsible for his condition, I could make a Vahazar from any man. Why do I say 'man'? From a hyena; from a jackal, even from a bedbug. It's all the same to me. – It's only a question of time. The disintegration of psychic atoms has started.

MORBIDETTO
Let's not talk about the future. If we could only get out of here, we'd have enough time to talk about it. The fact is that Vahazar is only a stupid illusion. I spit on Vahazar. You hear me?

SWINNY
You so-and-so! He brought you up from nothing.

FATHER UNGUENTE
She's right. We don't know what's in store for us. I withdraw into my wisdom like a snail into its shell, and I wait. I've waited so long, I can wait a little longer.

(He pulls his cloak over his head and seems to

fall asleep)

SWINNY
They're all lying. How strange! I feel so old! I believe my grandpapa will win.

RIPMANN
Madame Scabrosa, please control your child. I've had enough of that nonsense.

SCABROSA
That's nothing to do with me. Swinny is Vahazar's Lady-in-waiting. My life is finished. I'm quite prepared to become the mistress of the successor . . .

(She pulls a blanket over her head)

MORBIDETTO
Let's revolt! Let's plan a new life! Father Unguente, you and I shall create a monstrous double thundermitre.

FATHER UNGUENTE
(under cloak)
Not for the time being. I don't really know. Just at this moment I despise you.

MORBIDETTO

(to everyone)

I tell you, let's organize a prison rising. Let's go out into the streets with the slogan LONG LIVE WHOEVER IT IS! Perhaps we have been overlooked. Let's remind the world of our existence. Who will follow me?

SWEETY

I will. I belong to the male section. It's all the same to me.

FATHER UNGUENTE

(under cloak)

Stop! stop! I see what's going to happen!

SWINNY

(sitting on floor beside FATHER UNGUENTE)

We shall stay here, you and I. I believe Grandpapa will win through. He's good; he's only got a little mad. It's not the right time to talk to him now: he wouldn't understand.

MORBIDETTO

(bangs on door)

Hey! Open the door.

(Door opens, revealing QUIBOOZDA)
We want to get out! In the name of Vahazar's successor.

QUIBOOZDA

Of course you want to get out. Who *wouldn't* want to get out of jail?

MORBIDETTO

O don't joke about it, Quiboozda. Let us out. We'll take Vahazar with us and make a gift of him to his successor.

RIPMANN

Mr. Quiboozda: do tell us what happened.

QUIBOOZDA

Well, nothing. Everything is in order.

SCABROSA

Dear Mr. Quiboozda! It's not nice to keep us here. Please let us go! Please. All of us really hate Vahazar. Truly, I'm serious.

MORBIDETTO

Never mind about imploring him. Let's just push pasty, if this idiot won't stand aside.

(Elbows QUIBOOZDA in stomach and pushes through. Simultaneously, VAHAZAR's roar is heard. MORBIDETTO is pushed back into the cell, and the guards appear, led by BINDEN-GNUMBEN, in the doorway)

VAHAZAR

To think that anyone would jail *me*. You miserable navelstrings! you spiritual cripples! Me in a prison! Ha ha ha! What ripping fun! I forgive everybody!

(BINDEN-GNUMBEN enters with guards)

BINDEN-GNUMBEN

All the necessary orders have been carried out.

(He salutes)

VAHAZAR

(takes out revolver; in a breezy, jolly spirit)

Here is your reward.

(Shoots BINDEN-GNUMBEN dead)

Lubrica! Scabrosa! I shan't turn you into femaloons after all. You can be what you like.

(to RIPMANN)

Dr. Ripmann, you can continue with your laboratory research, but be a little more careful.

(to SWINNY)

You, my child, will remain a lady-in-waiting.

(to FATHER UNGUENTE)

I'll take you into partnership: 'Vahazar, Unguente and Company!' What d'you say?

SWINNY

(to SCABROSA)

Mama, didn't I say Grandpapa would be converted to the new faith?

(SCABROSA embraces her)

LUBRICA

And what of me?

VAHAZAR

O be what you like. Only let *me* alone.

(to FATHER PUNGUENTE)

As for you, Father Punguente, you are a mere cipher in this affair; so go on being a cipher, together with your Horizontalists.

FATHER PUNGUENTE

A million thanks, Your Lenity, for this imprisonment. I've been able to concentrate on inventing a new sect. This new sect is in fact–

VAHAZAR

Tell me later.

(to FATHER UNGUENTE)

Father Unguente, do come along for the final conference.

FATHER UNGUENTE

(still horizontal on the stretcher)

Yes. Why not?

VAHAZAR

Fine. Now let's go to the banquet. – Swinny, give me your hand.

SWINNY

My own grandpapa! I knew you'd be converted!

VAHAZAR

But what have I been converted to? Eh?

SWINNY

You'll find out later. Now let's go.

VAHAZAR

Hey! Verticalists! Take your Dundermitre and carry him to the palace.

(to the GUARDS)

Attention. March! Left, right, left, right, left, right.

MORBIDETTO
(running after VAHAZAR)
Your Ultrabuggery! Shall I be allowed –

VAHAZAR
(halts momentarily)
The more dangerous you are, my dear, dear Morbidetto, the more I like you.
(MORBIDETTO kisses his hand)
But you're not to torture anybody any more. You can only torture *me*. All right?

MORBIDETTO
Oh! I can't contain myself! Oh! What ecstasy!
(Jumps for joy)
Such a mad farce, all this!

VAHAZAR
Tut tut: don't exaggerate! Now let's go.

(VAHAZAR goes out with SWINNY; all follow)

CURTAIN

ACT 4

The same room as in Act One. Between the columns hangs an enormous yellow banner with the words in red letters: "Long Live Vahazar and Father Unguente!" and in bigger letters: "THE CONVERSION OF VAHAZAR!" and "CELEBRATION". On the right a black throne decorated with yellow stars. On the steps to the throne FATHER UNGUENTE is standing with a wide yellow ribbon across his chest. Women dressed as in Act One.

FATHER UNGUENTE

(rapping stick on floor to command silence)

You beggars of the spirit, who have buried your faith in the cemetery of shabby raptures! There's only one great truth. And only one faith flows from that truth. Down with intuition! Down with all instinctive cognition! Down with every form of intellectual humbug! I greet you in the name of the immediate future. The extent of my knowledge is terrifying. What I need is a generator of energy to give power to that knowledge. I nominate Vahazar, my partner in building the new world, as my generator.

FEMALE VOICE
(in crowd)
What a stale metaphor!

FATHER UNGUENTE
(rapping stick on floor again)
Quiet there! I've recovered from my bone ache thanks to the excellent Dr. Ripmann, who, incidentally, has been converted to our faith.
(He bows to RIPMANN, RIPMANN bows back)
Facts show that a personality can't be infinite, and that's why, in all highly developed species, individual entities combine to form large dung-balls, mmm, ant-hills, mmm . . . as I said, dung-balls without a faith, even without a notion of the mystery of the Total Existence. I don't see any sign of understanding in your faces.

(mixed noise from the crowd)

MORBIDETTO
May I ask, Father, what is Total Existence?

FATHER UNGUENTE
Total Existence may be either an individual existing existence or an organisation of existing existences into one existing existence . . . Either – or . . .

FEMALE VOICE
(from crowd)
What a bore! A warmed-up stew of dead ideas!

FATHER UNGUENTE
Silence there!

MORBIDETTO
Nobody can believe in an either/or.

MALE VOICES
(from crowd)
There must be a single definition.

FATHER UNGUENTE
(spreading arms)
Create your own sect and you may provide a single definition. There'll be no opposition to

it. Vahazar agrees with me on this.

VOICE
(from crowd)
To what sect does Vahazar belong?!

FATHER UNGUENTE
Vahazar and I are high above them all. But only the highest spirits can share the same peaks. The choice of one peak doesn't conflict with many-peaked truth. In this lies the superiority of faith based on pure Knowledge. We shall soon start evening classes, where everything will be explained.

VOICE
(from crowd)
Crap! This is not a school! We came here to celebrate!

FATHER UNGUENTE
I understand your feeling for glittering nonessentials and I shall gratify it presently. I shall sing you a song. But at this moment I wish to give the platform to the Great Doctor Joseph Jeremy Ripmann!

RIPMANN

Ladies and Gentlemen, Males and Females!

(Noise of surprised voices from crowd)

Up to now we were changing people's personalities by order, according to a total plan. Now we shall create the conditions in which the individualisation of glandularisation will allow everyone to become what he chooses to become within the limits of the cerebro-spinal system. We may even create new glands. Who knows? I am very happy and you are very lucky. Tomorrow there may be no difference between us. Do you understand? As from tomorrow – great wonderful muddle of transformatory possibilities! This is the miraculous truth I wanted to announce.

VOICES

(from crowd)

Long live Ripmann! New glands! New life! Enough of mystical blah blah! Biological truth, hooray!

(etc., etc., ad lib)

RIPMANN

Thank Father Unguente. It's all his idea.

VOICES

Long live Father Unguente! WE – WANT – GLANDS! WE – WANT – GLANDS! WE – WANT – GLANDS!

(RIPMANN and FATHER UNGUENTE bow to each other. QUIBOOZDA enters in a red uniform and yellow hat)

QUIBOODZA

(announcing)

Their Ineffabilities Vahazar and his Spiritual Daughter Swinella Macabrescu!!!

(Orchestra behind scene strikes up a military march, Vahazar enters dressed as a Verticalist with a yellow band across his chest. On his arm, Swinny dressed as in Act Three with a yellow veil on her head and a bouquet of pink roses)

VAHAZAR

(very loud voice – to SWINNY)

All right, all right. If we have to get through it, let's proceed.

SWINNY

(as loud)

Be calm, Grandpapa, I'm with you.

(Orchestra stops halfway through a bar)

VAHAZAR

Thank you, my child. I'm bored stiff.

(MORBIDETTO takes out of his pocket a large rope and stands in the doorway)

SWINNY

Tell them to stand at ease, Grandpapa.

VAHAZAR

Haaaaaaaa! Stand at ease!

(to FATHER UNGUENTE)

You can begin your number, Professor.

FATHER UNGUENTE

All right then. –

(Sings in a shaking voice)

Here am I. Here is he.
Bells toll
In my soul
Or gently tingling in me.
Sisters and sons, come over to me!
We are two. I am one.
This is Eden: softest down

Eden-down and eiderdown,
Poppies, pansies, on the lawn
Change their blossom with the dawn.
Motion stops in Acheron.
Punch the paunch!
Punch the paunch!
Truth is waiting
Scintillating,
Multiply equivocating.
Up from the depths a breath I've thrown!
Moss on the kernel of Truth has grown!
Where echoes mark a darksome hush
I drained my cup in one long flush.
Ascend, ye wraiths, and many a seer!
A corpse is here! A corpse is here!
Whenas the soul has met her doom,
Pluck the corpse of its every plume.
But see! The soul, from top to toe
Begrimed, bedunged, will hardly show
Even enough to wake the flesh
And make it start its life afresh.
Buy that flesh then, on the cheap!
The guardian's growling in his sleep.
Pick at the kernel of the supernal
Though panic selling of Truth eternal
For next to nothing should ensue.
Work then! Strive then! It's good for you

(Speaking voice)

Forgive me, all of you. I'm a philosopher, not a poet. I improvised that little poem as well as I could. Kneel down, Vahazar, and thus symbolize your union with eternal truth. And you, Swinny, innocent child of a perverted lust, kneel as well.

(VAHAZAR and SWINNY kneel)

VOICES

(from crowd)

This is a disgusting farce!

(Bell heard from behind stage. FATHER UNGUENTE kisses VAHAZAR and SWINNY on the forehead. Bell stops ringing)

FATHER UNGUENTE

That's enough celebrating.

(Turns to VAHAZAR)

Now listen to *me*, Vahazar. Your character is that of the lowest comedian, to whom the most immoral emperors would yield the palm for pervertedness and degeneracy.

VAHAZAR

If only it were so . . .

FATHER UNGUENTE

You want to humiliate me and disable me with your candour. Very well: you are nothing – you and all your predecessors – the only hope is that my idea will prevail. You understand: you're just not there. You don't exist.

VAHAZAR

I cannot quite subscribe to your reasoning. The fact is though that this is the strangest moment in my life. I simply don't know who I am.

FATHER UNGUENTE

I've won! I've won! You don't exist! *Tell* me you don't exist. Give me that satisfaction.

(VAHAZAR gets up)

VAHAZAR

To say I don't exist is not enough. I am a state of indescribability. It seems I'm everything. Kill me – or I'll die of self-admiration. What happiness! What delight!

SWINNY

(getting up)

Grandpapa! Grandpapa!

(She stands transfixed)

You're too beautiful!

FATHER UNGUENTE

(confidentially signaling to MORBIDETTO)

Now! . . .

(MORBIDETTO runs to VAHAZAR and throws the noose of his rope over his head. VAHAZAR falls back and dies. SWINNY throws herself on VAHAZAR's corpse)

SWINNY

He was my only love.

(Puts her arms round him. Holds pose)

FATHER UNGUENTE

That's that. We are free. – Dr. Ripmann, please cut out those glands while they are still warm; you know: carioxitates ripmanni – and prepare their secretions for *me*. Ripmann! Get a move on!

(He whistles on two fingers. The GUARD comes in)

SCABROSA
(goes up to SWINNY)
Poor poor child!

FATHER UNGUENTE
Morbidetto, now you are mine; *you* will be my generator – and my relaxation.

(RIPMANN stands looking balefully at the group)

MORBIDETTO
Yes, Your Homosexuality! All that went before was only a prelude to the really essential things.

FATHER UNGUENTE
O how happy I am! My youthful spirit, among the non-Euclidean tensions of multidimensional amorphous space. Come, Morbidetto. We shall now work out a synthesis of the *nonsense* of Vahazar and the *sense* of my absolute truth.

(MORBIDETTO leers)

FATHER UNGUENTE
Dr. Ripmann, don't gape at that sentimental

little scene, but get back to your speciality: glands.

(FATHER UNGUENTE and MORBIDETTO go out)

RIPMANN

(to SCABROSA and SWINNY)

Excuse me, ladies. I have to do my duty while the tissue is still alive. In a quarter of an hour it may be too late. And to have cut it out *while* he was alive would have killed him.

SCABROSA

(getting up)

Dr. Ripmann, don't be cruel! It was her *father*! That's why she's in such despair.

SWINNY

(gets up suddenly; indifferent)

Oh! was he? I didn't know. I thought it was pure accident that I loved him so much. But, if he was my father, I don't care. Take him, Ripmann.

RIPMANN

Strange are the ways of the subconscious. I wonder if glands could be of any help here.

(to GUARD)
Please take him His Late Imperishability to my biochemical laboratory.

(GUARD takes body out)

FATHER UNGUENTE
(returns with MORBIDETTO)
Dr. Ripmann: the spiritual perversity of this scoundrel is fathomless.
(indicating MORBIDETTO)

RIPMANN
The curse of the great ones of this world is that they always find some louse to suck their blood. Anyway, I have no time to discuss the little technicalities of life.

(He goes)

FATHER UNGUENTE
Don't forget the injection Dr. Ripmann. I'm spent. I'd like to be with some stranger, some simple person, beside whom I might rest.
(to FATHER PUNGUENTE)
And you, Father Punguente, what does your intuition tell you at this moment?

FATHER PUNGUENTE

Kill that girl.

(points at SWINNY)

FATHER UNGUENTE

Excellent! You'll be for me what I had to be for Vahazar.

(FATHER PUNGUENTE throws himself on SWINNY and tries to strangle her)

MORBIDETTO

Aha! Now I see the utter superiority of the new dispensation: the complete overcoming of all scruples. Bravo!

LUBRICA

(runs in with a dagger in her hand and hands it to SWEETY)

Kill him, Sweetoslav, show them what you're capable of!

(SWEETY throws himself on FATHER PUNGUENTE and impales him on the dagger. FATHER PUNGUENTE falls down dead. HORIZONTALISTS catch SWEETY by the arms)

SWINNY
(getting up)
Thank you, Sweety. I shall adopt you.
(to HORIZONTALISTS)
Let him go!

SWEETY
Ugh! I'm giving up the male section. I'm yours!
(SWINNY kisses him on the forehead)

FATHER UNGUENTE
(bewildered)
Now, what's this? What does it mean?

MORBIDETTO
Don't be afraid. This is one of those coming problems. They are our adversaries of the future. Let them be. Everyone has to have adversaries to be noticed at all.

FATHER UNGUENTE
You are probably right, Morbidetto. You're a wonderful theorist.

(SWINNY holds SWEETY in her arms, he weeps)

RIPMANN

(his head round the door)

I have Vahazar's glands here on my palm.
Still warm. Please, hurry, Your Injectability.

FATHER UNGUENTE

(hurrying out)

Is it not too late? I'm rather anxious.

MORBIDETTO

Run, you old carcass, nothing is ever too late . . .

SWINNY

Don't cry Sweety. One day we'll show them.

SWEETY

Yes, we'll show them. I shall be strong . . .
Like Grandpa Vahazar, like Father Unguente . . .

SWINNY

(putting her arms round him)

All right, all right. But come along now and play with me and my dolls.

(They go out)

SCABROSA

(following SWINNY and SWEETY with her eyes)

Poor mites!

QUIBOOZDA

(approaching her)

They'll be all right, ducky. They'll grow, they'll change, they'll adapt themselves . . .

(warmer)

They may even be given some brand new injections . . .

(passionately)

Old Ripmann is sure to invent some new thingumajig for them . . .

(Puts arm round SCABROSA and kisses her on the mouth. At back of stage three EXECTIONERS, two HORIZONTALISTS and four VERTICALISTS begin to laugh wildly)

SCABROSA

(yielding to QUIBOOZDA)

Ah-h-h! Even so . . . with the death of Vahazar all the charm of life has gone forever.

CURTAIN

14th November 1921

APPENDIX

VAHAZAR: A FEW SUGGESTIONS FOR DESIGN

by Franciszka Themerson, 1967

Décor – Art Nouveau – mostly white, grey and black; some gold.

Crowd of petitioners in the high fashion of the 1920s. Hats, outsized wigs, Lubrica carries a white lace parasol. In the Second Act, Swinny carries a huge painted balloon resembling Vahazar. In the Third Act, Lubrica and Scabrosa appear in gentlemen's white suits. In the Fourth Act, the ballroom is decorated as a fairground: awnings, platforms, little flags, oily primary colours, funny hats etc. With voices from audience.

All characters: white, black and grey, except Swinny and Sweety, very colourful, Carnaby Street style, boy long hair, girl blond lank hair falling over her face, mini-mini-skirt, lace tights.

Coloured lights* at the end of the play to be thrown on Quiboozda and Scabrosa reclining on an over-decorative sofa.

Voices from the crowd in Act Four come from actors among the audience.

Music?

* As used in floodlighting London's features of tourist interest.

SELECTED BIBLIOGRAPHY OF WITKACY

In Polish, the title of this play is *Gyubal Wahazar, czyli Na przełęczach bezsensu.* It was first published in a two-volume edition of twenty plays by Witkacy entitled *Dramaty*, edited by Konstanty Puzyna, PIW, Warsaw, 1962.

In 1972 Daniel Gerould published his English translation of this play as *Gyubal Wahazar, or Along the Cliffs of the Absurd: A Non-Euclidean Drama in Four Acts.* That translation is currently available in a collection called *Stanisław Ignacy Witkiewicz / Seven Plays,* Martin E. Segal Theatre Center Publications, New York, 2004. The Gaberbocchus translation by Celina Wieniewska Anglicized the title and the name of the main character, to wit, *Vahazar* (Polish Ws are pronounced as English Vs).

The first edition of Witkacy plays in English was *The Madman and the Nun and Other Plays*, translated and edited by Daniel C. Gerould and C.S. Durer, University of Washington Press, Seattle and London, 1967. The Themerson Archive, recently transferred to the National Library in Warsaw, contained a copy of this book. Applause Books (New York and London) reissued this collection in 2000 as two volumes, each containing three plays.

Daniel Gerould also edited and translated *The Witkiewicz Reader*, Northwestern University Press, Evanston, 1992. This is a compendium containing, amongst other Witkacy documents: four plays, two of which written by a juvenile Staś; excerpts from the novels *The 622 Downfalls of Bungo; or, The Demonic Woman,* and *Farewell to Autumn*; "Pure Form in Theatre;" "Rules of the S.I. Witkiewicz Portrait-Painting Firm"; and an excerpt from *Narcotics: Nicotine, Alcohol, Cocaine, Peyote, Morphine, and Ether.*

Witkacy's expansive final novel, *Insatiability,* was translated into English by Louis Iribarne and published by Northwestern University Press, Evanston, 1996.

ABOUT THE AUTHOR

Stanisław Ignacy Witkiewicz (pen name: Witkacy) was a Polish playwright, novelist, painter, photographer, and philosopher. Serving in the imperial Russian army, he was an eyewitness to the revolutionary upheavals in St. Petersburg in 1917. After returning to Poland, Witkacy supported himself painting portraits while he wrote over twenty plays between 1918 and 1924. VAHAZAR (1921) exemplifies both his "Pure Form" style and essential themes. He later wrote two dystopian novels. Finding himself trapped between invading armies of Nazis and Soviets, Witkacy committed suicide in 1939. With the passage of time, he is now recognized as a central figure in the Polish avant-garde.

Selected BLACK SCAT BOOKS

THE SQUADRON'S UMBRELLA
Alphonse Allais

CAPTAIN CAP: HIS ADVENTURES, HIS IDEAS. HIS DRINKS
Alphonse Allais

SELECTED PLAYS OF ALPHONSE ALLAIS
Compiled & translated by Doug Skinner

COMIC BOOK
Alain Arias-Misson

DANTE'S FOIL & OTHER SPORTING TALES
Mark Axelrod

THE ZOMBIE OF GREAT PERU
Pierre-Corneille Blessebois

SWEET AND VICIOUS
Suzanne Burns

AN INCONVENIENT CORPSE
Jason E. Rolfe

FISHSLICES
Paul Rosheim

THE DOUG SKINNER DOSSIER
Doug Skinner

CROCODILE SMILES: SHORT SHRIFT FICTIONS
Yuriy Tarnawsky

THE STRAW THAT BROKE
Tom Whalen

IMPOSSIBLE CONVERSATIONS
Carla M. Wilson

27216244R00076

Printed in Great Britain
by Amazon